HOLY BOLDNESS

HOLY BOLDNESS

by

Fr. Jack Spaulding

PUBLISHING COMPANY
P.O. Box 220 • Goleta, CA 93116
(800) 647-9882 • (805) 692-0043 • Fax: (805) 967-5133
www.queenship.org

Cover art:
Christ Driving the Money Changers from the Temple, ca 1570
El Greco, Spanish (born Greece), 1541-1614
The William Hood Dunwoody Fund
The Minneapolis Institute of Arts

Library of Congress Number # 2003095089

Published by:
Queenship Publishing
P.O. Box 220
Goleta, CA 93116
(800) 647-9882 • (805) 692-0043 • Fax: (805) 967-5133
www.queenship.org

Printed in the United States of America

ISBN: 1-57918-237-2

Table of Contents

This book
is dedicated to Mary,
Queen of the clergy
and to
my brother priests
in our
Jesus Caritas Faternity

August 22, 2003

Books like Holy Boldness do not come along often enough. It is a book that will be helpful for those who are discerning a vocation to ordained ministry as well as those who are already in programs of formation or serving in religious life. It helps "them" to find their calling (to diocesan or religious life) and it reminds "us" why we are being called. I would encourage those with a desire for "holy boldness" to read this book!

I especially enjoyed Father Spaulding's insight on page sixty-four of the text. He wrote that "when he, [the parish priest], relies on his 'grace of office' and trusts in the Lord, that He is never outdone in generosity, he is really allowing the Lord to use him in ways that the priest, himself, may have never dreamed of." Even as a bishop I have witnessed the truth of those words.

Faithfully in Christ,

Most Reverend Timothy M Dolan
Archbishop of Milwaukee

INTRODUCTION

Before you read this book you have the right to know the background of the author and, more importantly, the reason it was written. I am what some priests call a "lifer." This rather Gnostic term is used to denote someone who went to the seminary right after graduating from the eighth grade and continued in the seminary, through the college and theology divisions, until he was ordained. For a diocesan priest, like myself, that means I was in the seminary for twelve years. After graduating from St. Thomas the Apostle elementary school in Phoenix, Arizona, four other fellow graduates and I went to Regina Cleri Minor Seminary (high school) in Tucson, Arizona. The year was 1959, one year before the Second Vatican Council was convened by Blessed Pope John XXIII. I am now 58 years old, have been ordained for 32 years, am still serving in the Diocese of Phoenix, 23 of those 32 years as pastor. My current assignment is founding pastor of St. Gabriel's parish in north Phoenix. Also, I wanted to be a priest since I was in the second grade. I include this information because my vocation to the priesthood did not come from some "conversion of life," or after trying for years to avoid it. It, my vocation, was just there. My family is of the "cradle Catholic" variety, i.e., all were baptized Catholic as infants, as was I; but we didn't have any priests or religious sisters or brothers as relatives. Neither did my dad or mom ever suggest that I think about becoming a priest. I say these things to let you know that that day in second grade, in Sr. Rose Virginia's class at Sacred Heart grade school in Indianapolis, Indiana, the very convincing thought came to me that being a priest was what I wanted to do with my life. Nothing dramatic happened that day, no exterior vision or interior voice. I simply knew that is what I would be when I grew up. When people ask me now after all these years why I wanted to be a priest, my answer is the same with the addition of "...and this is what I believe God is still calling me to be."

After graduating from the minor seminary, my class was sent to St. John's Seminary College and Theologate in Camarillo, California, because we have no major seminary in Arizona. On June 25th, 1971, I was ordained a priest for the Diocese of Phoenix with two others, one also for the diocese, the other for the Jesuits. During my time as a priest for the Phoenix Diocese, I have served as associate pastor, founding director of the Office for Special Services for the Disabled, parish administrator, pastor, member of the Priests' Council, of the Diocesan Pastoral Council, Consultor to the Bishop, and as Chancellor of the Diocese, and was vice president of Life Teen International. I have been involved with World Wide Marriage Encounter, with the Cursillo Movement, and with Life in the Spirit Seminars. In 1980 I returned to school to get my master's degree in educational administration and supervision from California State University in Northridge, and in 1994 I went for continuing education at the North American College in Rome. A diocesan priest like myself is really the "general practitioner" of the priesthood, who is attached to a particular area, diocese, serving under the local Ordinary, the bishop of that diocese.

Now, why a book about the spirituality of a diocesan priest? Again, a little background may help with the answer. The majority of diocesan priests are trained in seminaries which are run either by one of the Religious Orders, e.g., the Benedictines, or one of the Religious Congregations, e.g., Salesians or Vincentians. Because of this, the seminarians are trained in the spirituality and prayer of the particular Order or Congregation. This formation is vital and valuable. However, once the seminarian becomes a diocesan priest, the spirituality and prayer forms that he experienced in the seminary will not be nurtured or even found in a diocesan parish setting. The typical diocesan parish to which the newly ordained priest is assigned may have only one other priest. Therefore, the sense of priestly community, which he had experienced all through his seminary career, is rare, and sometimes, nonexistent. So, it is a rather rude awakening for the newly ordained to discover that there is no one calling him to prayer or to meditation or to spiritual reading. Spiritually, he is basically on his own. What happens to his spirituality? Many times, as he becomes so busy, often overwhelmed, with the new and exciting responsibilities of being a parish priest, the first thing to go is his prayer time. He learns how to become professionally spiritual, celebrating the Sacraments for his people, especially Holy Mass and Reconciliation; but his personal spirituality begins to fade away. He can very easily succumb to the heresy that his work is his prayer. As his personal prayer time diminishes, he will eventually forget that he is "God's man for God's people." When this occurs it is a great loss for the Church and a great sadness because what people are looking for in their parish priest is a spirituality that makes God and His Presence in the world real for them. These words of St. Augustine ring loud and clear: "One cannot give what one does not have."

To say that there is *a* spirituality for diocesan priests is like saying that there is only one way of holiness for everyone. Obviously, this is not true. However, there are certain basic components to the spirituality of a diocesan priest, and, if these are lacking, his spirituality will become increasingly weaker. As this takes place he becomes less and less God's man for the people and more and more simply a man who tries to do good. In the following pages you will find the fundamental building blocks that compose the spiritual life of any diocesan priest. How the individual priest puts these together and lives them out certainly depends upon the grace of God and his co-operating with that grace. However, when you see a diocesan priest whom you consider to be a holy man of God for his people, these "spiritual stones" are well in place and are being lived out in his daily life. In this book, then, I hope you will find an insight into how your parish priest lives out his personal relationship with Our Lord Jesus Christ. My desire, also, is that the reader, whether you are a diocesan or religious order priest or lay person, will come away with a better understanding of what goes into the makeup of the spirituality of a diocesan priest. But, most of all, my hope is that, after reading this, you will continue to pray for your priests.

Prologue

The Difference Between Religious and Diocesan Priests

There are two ways of living out the vocation to the priesthood in the Church. The candidate chooses either to enter a religious order or congregation, for example, the Benedictines or the Jesuits, or to attach himself to a particular geographical area, a diocese. There are many different religious orders and congregations or societies, to name a few: Benedictines, Franciscans, Dominicans, Carmelites, Jesuits, Vincentians, Oblates of Mary Immaculate, Legionnaires of Christ, and the Missionaries of Charity. Each Order or Congregation was founded as specific needs developed in the Church. Some of these religious are basically teachers or missionaries; some are devoted to preaching or living together in a monastery for prayer and work. Some work specially with the poor. Each of these has a special "charism," or gift they bring to the service of the people of God. They "specialize" in a particular ministry. These priests, for the most part, live in community with their brothers. This community living is usually one of the things that attracts an individual to consider a religious vocation. These religious priests likewise take the vows of poverty, chastity, and obedience. In some Orders or Congregations there may be an additional vow, e.g., the Benedictines take a vow of stability, living in one monastery all their lives; the Missionaries of Charity, founded by Mother Teresa of Calcutta, take the vow of working with the poorest of the poor. Every Order or Congregation has its own specific spirituality, based usually upon that of its founders. The Jesuits follow that of St. Ignatius Loyola; the Franciscans, St. Francis of Assisi; the Vincentians, St. Vincent de Paul; the Missionaries of Charity, Mother Teresa of Calcutta; and the Dominicans, the spirituality of St. Dominic, to name just a few. Each is also supported by different forms of prayer and rules for living in his particular community. The living out of the priesthood for a religious order priest is flavored and supported by the particular religious community to which he belongs.

The priest who belongs to a religious order or congregation is attached to a particular Province, or geographical location. In the United States a religious Province could include several states, for example, the Franciscan Province of Santa Barbara consists of several western states. The religious priest is directly under the superior of the individual house, community, in which he lives and is ultimately under the direction of and obedience to the head of the particular Province. This priest is called the Provincial. In any Province there are usually several different dioceses, for example, the Diocese of Phoenix in Arizona, under the guidance and authority of a bishop. Although the religious priest has a vow of obedience specifically to his Provincial and receives his assignment from him, he serves in a particular area of the country at the pleasure of and in co-operation with the local diocesan bishop. For the most part there is a good relationship between the Bishop and the Provincial, as well as between the diocesan and the religious priests working in the same area of the country.

The second way of living out the vocation to the priesthood is for the individual to attach himself to a particular area of a state, for example, the Diocese of Phoenix in Arizona or the Diocese of Brooklyn in New York. A diocesan priest, also called a "secular" priest, meaning that the priest is not a member of an Order or Religious Congregation, does not take vows, as does a religious order priest. He makes the solemn promises of chastity, i.e., celibacy, and obedience to the diocesan bishop. The diocesan priest, contrary to popular opinion, does not take a vow of poverty. He receives a salary, a car allowance, stipends for celebrating Holy Mass, and a living allowance. The amounts of these items differ with each diocese and are usually determined by the local bishop with advice from the diocesan priests' council. The diocesan priest, likewise, pays state and federal taxes; and the majority of these priests pay into Social Security. One of the main challenges that a diocesan priest faces is that he is a "secular" priest. This term not only denotes that he belongs to a diocese rather than an Order or Religious Community, but it also reminds him that he is living *in* the world. He is challenged daily with not becoming *of* the world. Jesus, Himself, prayed for his Apostles at the Last Supper (John 17:9-19) that they avoid this ever-present temptation. The diocesan priest constantly needs to guard against being influenced by the values and priorities set by our society. He constantly needs to be aware of the subtle, and sometimes not so subtle, urge to be the "nice guy" and tell people what they want to hear instead of what they need to hear. He needs to constantly keep a check on how he uses his possessions so that he does not turn into a wealthy "bachelor." (We will look into this subject later in this book when we consider the diocesan priest's promise of celibacy.) The Order priest is not immune from the same temptations and challenges. However, because he is more "in" the world, the diocesan priest is more susceptible to being lured by them into a lifestyle that is not in keeping with his vocation. Usually a diocesan priest serves in a parish community. Depending upon the needs of a diocese, he could also teach in a diocesan high school or serve as a chaplain to a hospital or prison in his diocese. He can be assigned anywhere in the diocese where his bishop may need him. He would not be assigned outside of the diocese without specific permission from his bishop. The diocesan priest does not live "in community." He may live with another priest in the rectory belonging to the parish in which he serves; or, as is the case in many dioceses in the United States, he may live alone in his own apartment or house. Either way there is no "rule" of life or specific regimen or time set aside for prayer. In fact in many parishes in most of the dioceses in the country, there is only one priest. Having more than one priest in a parish is becoming the exception. For a diocesan priest there is no specific "charism," specific ministry. He is, as I said earlier, the "general practitioner" of the priesthood. Especially if he is assigned to parish ministry, the diocesan priest is in "family practice." The main responsibility of a diocesan priest is to assist the people, in the parish to which his bishop has assigned him, by preaching and teaching and celebrating the Sacraments to realize their eternal salvation—to help them get to heaven! And in doing this, to work out his own way to heaven.

As you can see, the life of a diocesan priest is far less structured most of the time than is the life of a religious order priest. The diocesan priest belongs to a diocese, is obedient to his bishop, and is usually assigned to a parish for his ministry. His spirituality is definitely different from that of his counterpart in a religious community. What comprises the spirituality of a diocesan priest? How does he live it out in his daily life?

Chapter One

Prayer— Public and Personal

Public Prayer:

The diocesan priest certainly needs to be a man of prayer. This is one of main reasons for which he is ordained, as is written in the Letter to the Hebrews, which is quoted in the Rite of Ordination to the Priesthood, "he (the priest) is taken from among men to offer sacrifice not only for their sins but for his own sins as well." One of his primary tasks and responsibilities is to offer public prayer for the people. He does this, of course, especially when he celebrates the Sacraments. When the priest baptizes, through his words and actions in the Sacrament of Baptism, he brings the people baptized out of original sin and makes them a child of God and a member of His holy people for all eternity. When the priest absolves, through his words and actions in the Sacrament of Reconciliation, the penitent's sins are forgiven, and healing and reconciliation with God and His people once again become a reality. When the priest confirms (the bishop delegates the pastor as the extraordinary minister for this Sacrament in certain situations, e.g., the Easter Vigil or danger of death), through his words and actions in the Sacrament of Confirmation, the candidate receives the outpouring of the gifts of the Holy Spirit and is strengthened to share them with God's people. When the priest stands in the place of God and officially represents God's people as he witnesses the exchange of vows between a man and woman as they become one through the Sacrament of Matrimony, the relationship between those two people becomes not only holy and permanent but also they, themselves, become one of the Sacraments of the Church. When the priest anoints with the holy oil, through his words and actions in the Sacrament of the Sick, the infirm receive the healing which they most need from God at that time. And in a very special way, when the priest offers the Holy Sacrifice of the Mass, each time he celebrate the Sacred Mysteries of the Holy Eucharist through his words and actions, God, Himself, gives the Body and Blood, the Soul and Divinity of His Only Begotten Son, Jesus Christ, to His people to be Strength for the journey. The diocesan priest's whole ministry revolves around celebrating the Sacraments for his people. So, it is only logical, that his own spirituality need also to revolve around and be nourished by these same Sacraments.

As he celebrates each of the Sacraments for his

people, the priest needs to really pray them, not just "go through the motions and say the words." Was not that one of Jesus' main criticisms of the Jewish leaders, that they followed the letter of the Law but forgot why the letter was written? Part of living out his spirituality is preparing well for each sacramental celebration. It is very tempting, because of how busy he can become or because this is the "one-hundred millionth time" he has done whatever prayer experience he is about to do, for the priest just to "throw on the alb and get with the program." After he is a priest for 15 minutes, he knows how to "do" the Sacraments. How unfortunate for him, as well as for his people, when he just "does" them. Does God "show up" when his priest acts this way? Of course, because God is always faithful. But what may be very lacking and may be missed entirely by everyone, when such a thing happens, is a real experience of the Presence of God. The priest needs to take seriously the admonition the bishop gave him during his ordination ceremony to "believe what you read; teach what you believe and practice what you teach." These words have specific reference to Sacred Scripture and then to the celebration of the Sacraments, especially the Sacrament of the Holy Eucharist when the rite of ordination adds " and imitate what you handle." To prepare well to celebrate the Sacraments takes time. Time, which, he may judge, could be spent doing something else more pressing. When the priest devotes time in his schedule to go over the prayers, especially of the Mass, so that he will be able to really pray them instead of simply say them; when he takes the time and the care to prayerfully go over the readings from Sacred Scripture to be read during the Mass, so that he is not only familiar with the words but with the Word living in them which he is about to proclaim; when he prayerfully meditates upon that Word so that he can truly preach what God wants His people to hear, then he is also working on his spirituality. The fact is everyone can tell the difference between the priest, who is simply "going through the motions" and the priest, who is allowing God to truly use him as His instrument as he acts in *persona Christi,* in the Person of Christ. The priest who acts in the former way is fooling no one but himself. The priest who acts in the latter way is a gift to his people and a credit to the priesthood. And, God is never outdone in generosity! The priest who honors God, God will honor him. I saw a little plaque, hanging in the priests' sacristy of a parish I once visited which, I suppose, could be taken either as an admonition or as a goal for the priest who was about to celebrate Mass. On this plaque was written: "Priest of God, celebrate this Mass as if it were your first and as if it were your last." Enough said!

Because one of his primary duties is to be the "public pray-er" or "presider," it is, often, very tempting for the priest to "put it on automatic" when it comes to leading his people in prayer. Especially with the Holy Mass, given the declining number of priests, at least at the present time, it is not out of the question that a parish priest celebrates at least two if not three Masses each weekend. This is not counting the Saturday morning Mass and the wedding and maybe a funeral or two besides. The priest needs to remember that, although it may be the fourth Mass for him that day, for his people it will be their only Mass that day and for God it is still the Last Supper. Too often, for many different reasons, the parish priest involves himself in projects and ministries that can be attended to by others as he de-emphasizes his responsibility of being the chief leader of public prayer. As one of my theology professors in the seminary said often, "No one can say Mass like a priest!" Although that may sound very trite, it is <u>true</u>. Why else would someone want to be ordained to the priesthood, if not to celebrate the Sacraments, especially the Holy Mass, for his people? Everything else that a parish priest does can be done by someone else. Looking at this area of his life from a merely practical point of view, it is a fact that he touches 90% of his people in celebrating the Sacraments for them—again especially Holy Mass. Why would not he, then, spend the majority of his time preparing for this holy encounter with his people for his God? Even a simple thing such as blessing items for people can become a chore if he forgets the reason for which he was ordained: to make God's Presence real for His people and to bring His people closer to Him. This awesome part of the priest's vocation will remain central and important to him only if he supports this public prayer with his personal prayer time.

Personal Prayer:

As the parish priest prepares well for the celebration of the various Sacraments he provides for his people and as he also enters deeply into these sacramental actions of Divine Grace, his own spiritual life is strengthened and revitalized. However, if this public sacramental prayer ministry constitutes his only form of prayer, there is something lacking. This lack is his personal prayer life. Both a public and a personal spirituality are needed in the life of any follower of Christ. Both are vital in the life of a priest. In fact a priest cannot have a true public spirituality unless his personal prayer life is a healthy one. We priests need not kid ourselves into believing that our people cannot tell the difference between a priest who prayers and a priest who does not. When we are not prayerful in our private time, when we do not take time each day to work on our personal relationship with Our Lord, there is no way that we can hide that lack when we come to preside over the public prayer of the Church for our people. I would say that in the majority of cases of priests leaving the active ministry, the root cause can be traced back to the lack of a personal prayer life, to the lack of a personal spirituality. They were professionally spiritual but not personally spiritual. In a priest you cannot have the one without the other if he wishes to remain an active priest for the rest of his life.

So, what goes into the makeup of the personal prayer life of a diocesan priest? The following are basic forms of personal prayer and devotion that are available to everyone as well as to the priest. How each of these is used obviously will depend upon the individual. "One size" does not fit every diocesan priest's spirituality or his personal prayer life. That being said, however, these basic prayers and devotions have been used, are presently being used, and will continue to be used as the foundation of the personal spirituality of a diocesan priest.

Devotion to the Eucharistic Presence of Our Lord

Since the source and summit of the spiritual life of any Catholic Christian is the Holy Eucharist, it follows then that the center of a diocesan priest's personal spirituality necessarily is not only the celebration of Holy Mass but also spending time in adoration of Our Lord in the Most Blessed Sacrament. Our Holy Father, John Paul II, has encouraged each parish to have a perpetual adoration chapel so that everyone has twenty-four hour, seven-day-a-week, access to the Eucharistic Presence of Our Lord. Even if the parish in which the priest is assigned is unable to have an adoration chapel, Our Lord's Eucharistic Presence remains in the Tabernacle. The disciples were sent out by the Lord to spread His Word and to minister to the needs of the people. However, as we are reminded in the Scriptures, they would come back to Him, sit at His feet, and listen to Him speak to their hearts as they remained again in His Presence. If the disciples needed this time with Him in order to serve His people, as He wanted them to, then the parish priest is also in need of this kind of "quality, one-on-one time" with Our Lord. For the priest to often come before the Eucharistic Presence of Our Lord to not only present the needs of his people to Him but also to present his own needs and, maybe more importantly, to simply remain in His Presence to be healed and strengthened, and comforted, and to be reminded that he is not alone, that "you have not chosen Me but I have chosen you," is absolutely essential if his spiritual life is to be a healthy and dynamic one. How can a priest claim to be an *alter Christus,* another Christ, if he doesn't really know Him? How can he know Him if he doesn't spend time in His Presence? To come before the Lord and to sit or kneel quietly before the Holy Eucharist, puts everything into proper perspective. If his life is out of focus or his priorities have become mixed up, all will become clear again as the Light of the Son shines into the cluttered darkness and disarray of his heart and soul. This is where the "wounded healer" comes to be healed by the Doctor of his soul. Eucharistic adoration is where the one, who has been called to act in *persona Christi*, in the person of Christ, for the people, comes into the very real presence of the Person of Christ, Himself. What better way for the priest to be re-invigorated and re-energized for his ministry? And what better way to remind himself of not only why he is doing what he is doing but also, and most importantly, for whom? When the priest comes into the Presence of his Eucharistic Lord, it is the disciple coming back to the Master. As he sits or kneels or lies prostrate before his God, the priest remembers who he is; he remembers why he is; he remembers to whom he belongs; he remembers to whom he has been given; and he remembers why he has been given to them. The time the priest spends in adoration of the Blessed Sacrament will not only strengthen his own spirit but it will also help him to be more compassionate and merciful to his people. It is very obvious to his people when their priest takes advantage of this Eucharistic devotion. It is also obvious when he does not!

Devotion to the Sacred Scripture

Going hand in hand with devotion to the Holy Eucharist, the diocesan priest's personal spirituality is fed and strengthened when he immerses himself in Sacred Scripture. The priest is the "proclaimer" of the Word of God to his people. Next to celebrating the Sacraments, again with a special emphasis on the Holy Mass, his most important responsibility as priest is to preach the Good News of Jesus Christ. How can he do this effectively and affectively unless that same Word permeates his very soul? There is a story told about an atheist who, for whatever reason, was a professor of theology at a large university. When his students discovered this about him. They asked how he could teach a subject the very core of which he did not believe? His reply was, "It's a paycheck and I fake it." If that professor was a good teacher, the students most likely learned the material, but there was probably not much inspiration imparted. Something similar can very well take place when the priest puts his preaching on "automatic" or when he simply takes out of his files the same sermon he preached on a particular Sunday three years ago. (As you know we are on a three-year cycle for the Scriptures proclaimed during Sunday liturgies.) This can and does happen when he does not devote himself to studying the Scriptures, but especially it can and does happen when he does not prayerfully read them often. This practice and devotion is called *lectio divina*, divine reading. To slowly and prayerfully read the words of the Sacred Scriptures so that the Word of God, contained within them, becomes clear, is essential to the priest's spiritual growth. His soul needs to be permeated with the Word. It needs to be as much a part of him as is his breath! Along with this *lectio divina* is the praying of the Liturgy of the Hours, or the Divine Office. This prayer originated in the monasteries and is designed to be prayed in common. This prayer, like the prayer of the Holy Mass, is an act of public worship, whether it is prayed by many people together or by an individual alone. The Liturgy of the Hours is comprised mostly of the Psalms and corresponds to the Holy Mass, which is celebrated on any particular day. When the Office is prayed in common, especially when it is prayed in a monastery, the psalms are usually sung. The "hours" consist of: the Office of Readings, Morning Prayer, Daytime Prayer, Midmorning Prayer, Midday Prayer, Midafternoon Prayer, Evening Prayer, and Night Prayer. The original purpose of Liturgy of the Hours was so that the Church would turn to God many times during the entire course of the day, keeping God central to all we do. That purpose persists to this day. Through the praying of the Divine Office, the Church continues to consecrate each hour of the day to God, the Giver of all time. More likely than not, the diocesan priest does not have the opportunity to pray all of the hours of the Office in common. Many times he is the only priest in the parish. What is the usual practice is that he prays Morning Prayer, Evening Prayer, and Night Prayer by himself. Many priests pray the Office of Readings together with Morning Prayer. The temptation is great for the parish priest not to pray the Office because it "really should be prayed in common," or the Office is "really the prayer of the monks." Granted, praying these prayers alone is not really the way the Church means for them to be prayed, they still constitute part of the public prayer of the Church. So whether the Liturgy of the Hours is prayed by many or by one it is still a public act of worship. It should be of great comfort to the parish priest, especially if he is alone, that when he prays the Office he prays with the whole Church for the whole Church. He is not praying alone. Praying the Holy Scriptures, as well as praying the Divine Office, will fortify the soul of the priest so that he will be able to speak and live the very Truth of God as revealed in Jesus Christ. Likewise, being steeped in the Word of God, his everyday life will be a living sermon of the mercy and compassion God shows to him and through him to his people. The parish priest will be an example of what St. Francis of Assisi meant when he said, "I preach the Gospel and sometimes I use words."

Meditation and Spritual Reading

Another "tool" which a parish priest uses to strengthen his personal spiritual life is meditation. In recent years with the surge in popularity of "reaching the inner self" and the self-actualization that goes hand in hand with the New Age movement, meditation has again come into its own. As we know this is not a new discovery for the Church. Down through the ages saint after saint has shown by example as well as by their writings the importance of meditation to anyone who wishes to make progress in his spiritual journey. Meditation is basically clearing the mind of external distractions as we concentrate on a particular subject that brings us to a clearer understanding or realization. It "centers" us and brings peace. For the Catholic Christian the "particular subject" is God Himself, and meditation brings us to a clearer understanding or realization about our relationship with Him or about one of His gifts, for example, His mercy or compassion. This form of prayer requires setting time aside for quiet reflection. Because of this requirement, meditation may be the most difficult kind of prayer for the parish priest. Many times he may feel "guilty" about taking time to simply "be" with the Lord when there are so many things that need to be done and so many people who need to be seen. Yet it is precisely this kind of prayer that really helps him help his people. The reasons for them coming to seek his counsel will be as many and as varied as the people themselves, but what they are all looking for, when they come to see their priest, is peace and an understanding merciful heart. Again, how can he give what he does not have? If he does not take the time for quiet meditation, the priest not only cheats himself but he also cheats his people. This form of prayer is vital for him so that he can remain "centered" on the Lord. Without meditation it is easy to quickly forget Who the center of his life needs to be. With meditation he continually reminds himself that he is God's man for his people.

Many times meditation and spiritual reading go hand in hand. Often spiritual reading is the catalyst for meditation. Spiritual reading is very different from reading that a priest does for information, or for preparing a class or sermon. The main purpose of spiritual reading is for inspiration—to feed the spirit, to nourish the soul. So a "spiritual reading" book needs to provide the kind of material that would inspire and nourish the priest's spirit. Books on the lives of the saints or on the virtues; the encyclicals; the writings of the saints; the Holy Scriptures, any of these falls into this category. This kind of reading gives encouragement to live a life of holiness. Like *lectio divina*, spiritual reading, requires a thoughtful reading of the subject matter, stopping when something hits the heart and allowing whatever that is to penetrate his soul. Again, because of the "time commitment" needed for this, it is easy for the priest to put this part of his spirituality at the bottom of the list, or to exclude it altogether. When this happens as when he forgoes meditation, the priest loses a great opportunity for spiritual growth and so his people will also lose. The stronger the parish priest's spirituality is, the stronger the spirituality of his people will be.

Reconciliation and Spirtual Direction

The phrase, "no man is an island," applies in a particular way to the parish priest in the areas of the Sacrament of Reconciliation and spiritual direction. In order for him to lead his people closer to the Lord, he, himself, must continually take a "spiritual inventory." He does this with the help of his confessor and spiritual director. Contrary to popular opinion, the priest does not stand in front of a mirror and give himself absolution. He, like every Catholic Christian, needs to come before the Lord, through the instrumentality of another priest, to confess his sins and seek healing and reconciliation by receiving the grace of this great sacrament. By being a penitent himself and realizing his own need for forgiveness, the priest's compassion for his fellow sinners becomes more a part of his life. The greatest confessor is the priest who knows that he also is a sinner in constant need of the merciful forgiveness of his God. The frequent use of this sacrament, at least every month, will help to weed out habitual sin and guard against serious sin. This "habit" of frequent reception of the Sacrament of Reconciliation, of course, is good for everyone. It is, however, essential for the priest. Without it, not only will his conscience become less acutely aware of the constant and subtle bombardment of the attacks of the devil upon his own life, but also he will not see the necessity of continually encouraging his people to make use of this Sacrament. When this happens the spiritual life of the parish is in jeopardy. Again, in this area as in all the other areas of the spiritual life, the parish priest needs to lead by example. How can he speak convincingly about the beauty and need for the Sacrament of Reconciliation for his people if it is not an integral part of his own spirituality? The fact is, if the priest does not frequent Reconciliation neither will his people because he will *not* speak about it. In the parishes where this sacrament is offered on a regular basis, sometimes even daily, you can be assured that the priest himself has made this sacrament an indispensable part of his own life.

One of the main responsibilities of the parish priest is to lead his people in the way of holiness. He does this in part through the homilies he preaches, by his own example, and, most specifically, through spiritual counseling. This is usually called spiritual direction. Spiritual direction involves entering into the spiritual life of people and assisting them in discerning what the Lord is doing in their lives and how He is calling them closer to Himself. People seek this type of direction in order to grow in their relationship with God and to receive an objective and unbiased view of what He is doing in their lives. If spiritual direction is helpful for the spiritual growth of the laity, it is essential for the spiritual growth of the parish priest. There is a great temptation for the priest, especially if he does a lot of spiritual direction, to believe that he really does not need this for himself. After all he is the "professional" in the area of spirituality and so he can discern things for himself. As I said, this is a great temptation! As the old saying goes, the one who has himself as a counselor has a fool as a counselor. A priest who is his own spiritual director is like a doctor who diagnoses his own ailments. Although the priest, especially a parish priest, may be the spiritual director for many—even for other priests, he himself needs to have his own spiritual director for the simple and undeniable fact that he cannot be objective with himself. He is too close to the situation many times to be able to take an honest look at what is happening and to see what needs to be done. A spiritual director for a priest is an indispensable tool for growth in his spiritual life. Without spiritual direction not only will his spiritual life go flat but it will, over a period of time, also deteriorate. Once this happens, his own ability to guide his people along the way of holiness will be impaired and he will eventually begin to give the people who come to him for spiritual guidance, not the prayerful discernment regarding God's action in their lives, but merely his own opinion based on "my years of experience." Again, he cannot give what he does not have!

Choosing a spiritual director is one of the most important decisions a priest will make because this is the person who will help guide him along his way to salvation. This may sound a little melodramatic, but, in fact, this is precisely the role of a spiritual director. The spiritual director becomes that "objective point of view" which is essential to the priest in his discerning God's action in his life. Because this relationship between the priest and his spiritual director is an ongoing one it is very important for the priest to select whom this will be with care. This person needs to be someone of integrity who has been and is actively working on his own spiritual development. The priest needs to be sure that his spiritual director has a spiritual director. This person also has to be someone with whom the priest is comfortable in sharing his thoughts, feelings, hopes, fears, and opinions. He needs to able to trust him. Most importantly, the priest must be willing to be challenged by his spiritual director and to truly listen to his spiritual advice. When we read any of the lives of the saints, we see that the role of their spiritual directors was critical to their progress in holiness. If that held true for them, it also holds true for the parish priest. Together with the frequent reception of the Sacrament of Reconciliation, meeting on a regular basis, perhaps quarterly, with his spiritual director will assist the priest in taking an ongoing "spiritual inventory" of his life. These will certainly help him keep his priorities in order and provide him with the ongoing opportunity to make changes or corrections in his life before a bad habit, either spiritual or material, can take root. Making proper use of Reconciliation and spiritual direction will act as "preventive medicine" for the spiritual life of the parish priest.

Devotion to the Blessed Virgin Mary and the Saints

Another facet of the priest's personal spirituality is his private devotions. These will complement and supplement all of the areas of the priest's spirituality we have already mentioned in the previous pages of this book. These devotions will be as many and as varied as the number of priests who use them, and so to enumerate them all would be an impossibility. There are, however, some basic categories of private devotions that can be looked at. Two of these are devotion to the Blessed Virgin Mary and to the saints.

The Blessed Virgin Mary: One of the titles given to the Blessed Mother is Queen of the Clergy. As she stood at the foot of the cross, Mary was given to all of us by her Son in the person of St. John. From that moment she became the Mother of us all. Her example of humility, being honest before the Lord, and obedience to God is something that everyone tries to emulate. The gentle command she gave to the waiters during the wedding feast at Cana in Galilee to "do whatever He asks," has been the same reminder she has given each time her Son has allowed her to visit us down through the ages. This reminder of putting God first and of seeking His Will, of course, is applicable to everyone's life. It has special meaning in the life of a priest. This is the reason that it is essential for him to have a great devotion and relationship with Mary. It is she who, in many of her apparitions, has spoken of the priests as her "beloved sons." It is she who, again in many of her apparitions, has stated that she constantly prays for priests. The priest who has true devotion to the Blessed Mother can never stray too far from her Son before her prayer brings him back. Praying the rosary, praying some of the litanies dedicated to Mary, participating in novenas which honor her can all be part of the priest's Marian devotion, but the most important thing the priest needs to do is grow in his relationship with her. He does this by prayerfully meditating on what the Sacred Scriptures say to us about her and by confidently going to her often, speaking to her as a child speaks to his own mother. In whatever situation or circumstance the priest finds himself in, no matter what temptation or challenge to his priesthood he may be going through, if he turns to Her for help, she will always lead him safely through the darkness to the Light of her Son. This is what she does. This is who she is. Mary is not only the Queen of the Clergy she is also their Mother! The priest, who does not have a devotion to the Blessed Mother or who may even belittle the need for it, is like a person who sets sail on the ocean without a life preserver. He is either too dumb or too arrogant to realize how vulnerable he is and so he tries to "go it alone." The consequences of this kind of bravado are disastrous for the sailor and for the parish priest. The simple prayer of Mother Teresa of Calcutta should never be far from the lips of any priest: "Mary, be a mother to me now!"

The Saints: As Catholic Christians we are blessed by the relationship we have with all of our brothers and sisters who have gone before us and who are now in heaven. In fact the number of canonized saints who populate the liturgical calendar of the Church is staggering. There are men and women of every circumstance and vocation we can imagine. All have responded to the call of holiness in their own life situations and have been rewarded by God and honored by the Church for their faithfulness to that call. So there is no lack of holy people for any of us to use as an example for our own lives and to call on for intercession as we try to live out that same call to holiness. For a priest to have devotion to the saints should go without saying. What he has to do is choose which of these great people he will have a special relationship with. For the parish priest, one of his special patron saints should be the one for whom the parish, he is assigned to, is named. That saint has a specific tie to the parish and, it seems only appropriate that, the priest should call upon that saint's intercession for the welfare of the parish, as well as his own, as he ministers to the people there. He should also remind his people of the special relationship they have with their parish's patron saint and encourage them to seek the saint's intercession in their lives. This connection with the Communion of Saints on the parish level, I think, is an overlooked and under-used means of grace both for the people and for the priest. For the parish priest two saints immediately come to mind as great patrons, Saint John Vianney and St. Therese of Lisieux. St. John was the parish priest of Ars in France in the 19th century. Because of his personal holiness, fueled by his devotion to the Blessed Sacrament and to the Blessed Mother, the parish of Ars was completely transformed and became, even in his lifetime, a place of pilgrimage. He spent untold hours in the confessional, bringing all who came to him there God's healing, forgiveness, and mercy through the Sacrament of Penance. Tens of thousands flocked to this out-of-the-way place to hear the saint speak of the central love of his life, the Real Presence of Christ in the Most Blessed Sacrament. The saint was tempted often and did literal battle with the devil. The stories of these encounters are numerous and demonstrate that, after a while, he began to understand that such attacks were the consequence of trying to live the way God was calling him and so he took it all in stride. What an example for the parish priest! St. John Vianney is truly someone who knows what it is like and what is required in living out the call of a parish priest.

St. Therese of Lisieux is not only a Doctor of the Church and the Patroness of the Missions but this young, cloistered, Carmelite nun also had a tremendous love for priests. In her autobiography, "The Story of a Soul," she writes about "adopting" two priests as her spiritual brothers and how she prayed and offered sacrifices for their faithfulness to their vocations. If she did that while she was here on earth, this prayer and intercession for priests is even more intense now that she is in heaven. Calling upon her in times of temptation or discouragement, following her example of living her "little way" of holiness in this complicated world of ours, and also, perhaps more importantly, following her example of loving those in our lives whom we consider the most unlovable, will go a long way in helping the parish priest be a true pastor, a good shepherd, for his people.

Together with these saints, the priest should always have a special spiritual relationship to his own patron saint/s, the one for whom he has been named and the one he chose at his Confirmation. Again, perhaps, much grace is lost and much spiritual assistance goes begging because the priest fails to call upon the intercession of these his special patron saints. Another source of spiritual help for him is his own guardian angel. This angel is given to him when he is baptized and stays with him throughout his life. What a shame and loss if the priest never calls upon the assistance of this his own messenger from God!

This whole area of prayer, both public and private, is central and essential to the spirituality of the diocesan priest. Without an active prayer life the parish priest will get swallowed up in the everyday busy-ness of parish life. As that happens he will gradually begin to focus on being an administrator, or builder, or organizer, or fund-raiser instead of dedicating himself to what he is called to be by his vocation to the diocesan priesthood, namely, the spiritual father and shepherd for the people to whom God has given him by the "laying on of hands" when he was ordained.

Chapter Two

DISCIPLINE AND DETACHMENT

The life, which the diocesan priest has chosen through his vocation to Holy Orders, has two distinctive characteristics: discipline and detachment. These are really pivotal aspects of his life as a diocesan priest. He lives them out through his obedience to the Church in the person of his bishop and by embracing a life of celibacy for the Church as a sign of Christ's Kingdom here and yet to come. Living a life of discipline and detachment to any degree is obviously counter-cultural these days. Living the kind of discipline and detachment to which a diocesan priest is called is not only looked upon as counter-cultural by society in general but it is also considered by most as impossible and by many as unnatural. So what is involved in this life of obedience and celibacy that the diocesan priest has committed himself to?

First, let us look at his solemn promise of obedience. In the ordination ceremony the deacon, who is about to be ordained to the priesthood, kneels before his bishop and, placing both of his hands in the hands of the bishop, answers, "Yes," when he is asked by the bishop himself, "Do you promise obedience and respect to me and to my successors?" With that "yes" the priest commits himself to living his life in a different way from that of anyone else. The obedience of a diocesan priest reflects the very obedience of Christ that St. Paul has immortalized in the beautiful hymn recorded in the second chapter of his letter to the Philippians. Quoting from this passage: "Have this attitude in you which was that of Christ Jesus (humility and obedience.)" This "attitude" changed the very course of human existence and won eternal life. Obedience is truly and ultimately the key to our eternal salvation. It is also, here on earth, the gift of true freedom. So the when the diocesan priest promises his bishop obedience and respect, he is simply dedicating his life to the pursuit of true freedom here and eternal salvation in the life to come. This really seems to be a "no brainer," but like everything else, which is of true value, living a life of real obedience has its challenges.

Obedience is basically turning your will over to another. When the priest makes this promise to his bishop, he commits himself and his life to following what is ask of him by the bishop, trusting that what will be asked, down through the years, will be for his own good and for the good of the diocese. What a step out in faith and trust this is! When the diocesan priests submits his will to that of his bishop he makes an implicit act of faith that his bishop and "his successors" have likewise committed themselves in obedience to God and to the Church. He trusts that his bishop will ask of him only what God would ask. This has so much to do with believing in the "grace of office." This grace of office is the gift which each bishop receives when he is ordained bishop and which each bishop, with God's help, takes very seriously. The bishop does not take this gift lightly, and neither should the priest. The priest himself, because of his ordination, receives this grace of office to fulfill his responsibilities in his parish, either as an associate or as pastor. How can he except and receive obedience and respect from his parishioners if they do not see him being obedient and respectful to his bishop? As we can see, this obedience and respect works both ways.

The grace, which comes with the promise of obedience he makes to his bishop, is that of being free to serve in whatever capacity and in whatever assignment his talents and the needs of the diocese may require. This "grace" also inoculates the priest against the "disease" of creating his own kingdom and prevents him from succumbing to the illusion that "this parish/work/agency/ministry will collapse if I am transferred." Obedience likewise allows the priest to give his whole heart and soul and energy to whatever assignment he is given no matter how long a time he may be there. One of the attitudes which goes against his living out this promise of obedience is: "I can't get too involved or start any new programs or ministries because I may not be here for very long and it would be unfair to the people if the next priest would not continue what I started." When the priest is truly living out this promise, his attitude is: "I need to do all the good I can while I am here. Whatever happens after I am gone is in God's hands." Holding back from using his God-given gifts just because he is uncertain about the length of his assignment calls into question not only his trust in God's providence but also may indicate a difficulty in committing himself totally to living in the present moment. Living a life of obedience gives the diocesan priest this gift of living fully in the present moment while trusting his future to the Lord.

Living this promise of obedience does not mean that the diocesan priest cannot express his thoughts to or ask questions of his bishop regarding a particular assignment. We need to give our blind obedience to the Lord alone. With everyone else we need to be able to sit down and talk. This "everyone" includes the priest and his bishop. In keeping with the dictates of the Second Vatican Council regarding consultation, dialogue, and collaboration, the bishop has the right to know what his priests are thinking, especially what their thoughts are about a particular assignment. Most bishops today consult, not only with a placement board that is usually composed of priests and others knowledgeable in the needs of the diocese and the talents of the priests, but also with the priests themselves, before an assignment is made. The priest has every right to let his bishop know his thoughts and feelings about an assignment before it takes effect. The days of the autocratic bishop have, gratefully, for the most part, come to an end. The bishops are few who still play "I'm the bishop and you're not" with his priests. Most would not give an assignment to a priest if he had legitimate objections to it. However, after discussing the pros and cons of any assignment, the diocesan priest's response needs to be: "Bishop, I have shared my thoughts and feelings about this with you. You need to know that I will be obedient to whatever you ask of me." What a gift of reassurance for the bishop and what a gift of freedom for the priest!

One of the accompanying benefits of his life of obedience is that it takes him out of church politics, which can bring spiritual as well as emotional harm to the priest and to his people, as well as cause him, over the years, much disappointment and frustration. Early on, the diocesan priest needs to decide whether he is going to be a priest or a clerical politician, whether the priesthood will be his life or his career. If he chooses the path of being a "career cleric," his whole life will be guided by knowing the right people, being seen in the right light, vying for the right assignment, and seeking out the patron who will advance him up the ecclesiastical ladder. This of course will require a lot of time and energy, and the emotional pressure will be tremendous. This kind of ambition can be, and most of the time is, very destructive and will eventually take its toll on his ability to truly minister to the needs of his people. When he does not receive the "right" assignment or when he is passed over for the "promotion," the chances for the priest to become devastated and embittered are extremely high. All of this can be avoided if he chooses the priesthood as his life. Obedience, first of all to the Lord and then to the Church through his bishop, helps the priest keep his priorities straight and his focus clear regarding the true reason he was ordained, to give all of his talents and energy back to the Lord in service to the people of his diocese. When he embraces obedience as the way he will live out his priesthood with his whole heart, the priest frees himself of destructive ambition and becomes, for the rest of his life, ambitious for the "higher gifts," as St. Paul writes in his first letter to the Corinthians. What a gift to his people, and to the Church, is the truly obedient priest!

We now take a look at the diocesan priest's solemn promise of celibacy. Celibacy, in the context of the Sacrament of Holy Orders, is a multi-faceted gift to the

Church and to the priest himself. Let it be said right up front that priestly celibacy has much more to do with a total giving of self than it has to do with giving up anything or anyone. Especially to our society at this present moment, anything that has to do with self-denial has absolutely no value particularly when this self-denial involves refraining from sexual activity, that is with the possible exception of using it as a respite when moving on from one genital relationship to another. As I said, if priestly celibacy is equated with giving up genital sexual relationships, including the monogamous relationship with a wife, and giving up the gift of bringing children into the world, then it not only has no meaning but it is also unnatural and, moreover, an impossible way to live. However, since priestly celibacy is not simply a "giving up" but rather a giving totally of oneself for others, this celibacy, which the diocesan priest solemnly promises to live, from the time he is ordained a deacon onward, becomes possibly the sign to the world that, as Sacred Scripture says, "God's ways are not our ways and God's thoughts are not our thoughts." Maybe today, more than ever, can this gift of celibacy, lived out daily by the diocesan priest, give hope and assurance to our increasingly pessimistic world, steeped in its culture of death, that "this is not all there is," that there is much, much more to us and for us than can be seen by the eye, heard by the ear, or touched by the heart, mind, or hand. This "more" is witnessed to when the priest embraces celibacy for his people and for the "sake of the kingdom of heaven." To forgo for his entire life the greatest physical gift given to us by our Creator, that of being husband and father, there has to be more involved in living this kind of a celibate life for the diocesan priest. And there is!

I think it needs to be understood that the requirement for priests to be celibate, as a condition for ordination, is a discipline of the Western or Roman Church and was discussed as early as 306 in Spain at the Council of Elvira. However, it was not established as a Church law until the First and Second Lateran Councils in 1123 and 1139 respectively. Mandatory clerical celibacy was reaffirmed during the Council of Trent in the 16th century. (As a matter of interest and clarification, the Eastern Rite Churches have a different tradition when it comes to priestly celibacy.) Because this mandatory celibacy for priestly ordination is a disciplinary law of the Church it could be changed. As of this writing, and most likely for the foreseeable future, this rule is still in place. I state the current situation for two reasons. First, there is, and continues to be, both public and private debate on the pros and cons of mandatory priestly celibacy. Second, and in my opinion most important and extremely critical, the reality for the diocesan priest is that, if he regards this requirement of mandatory celibacy as only a discipline, more than likely as the years go on, not only will his commitment to living a celibate life weaken but he will also lose sight of the true gift it could be to him. If he focuses only on the disciplinary aspect of celibacy, what will be lost to him is the overwhelming fact that God is never outdone in generosity. What I have seen happen for many priests, and can personally witness to, is that what began perhaps as only following a discipline of the Church can be and is transformed by God's grace, simply by asking for it, into a way of life which is fuller by far than anything they could have hope for or even imagined for themselves. This gift of celibacy is what we need to take a closer look at.

As was mentioned before celibacy is more about giving than about giving up. When the parish priest makes the promise of lifelong celibacy and truly embraces it as a gift from God to the people, what he does is enter into a new and different kind of relationship with everyone. In a life of consecrated celibacy the priest completely and totally dedicates all of who he is, body, mind, spirit, intellect, emotions, and even the way he spends his time, to God in service to God's people. With this comes a true freedom to be "God's man." Celibacy, lived as a gift, exemplifies the priest's utter dependence upon God to fulfill all his needs. He detaches himself from the usual and normal means of support, spouse and children, so that he can attach himself more completely to God and, through this "attachment," to all who need him. Through a life of celibate love the priest promises to belong to no one exclusively except God. As the phrase from an old reflection on the priesthood written by Lacordaire states: "(he) is part of every family but belonging to none."

Embracing a life of celibacy is, in reality, embracing a lifelong commitment to love God's people as Jesus loved them. Being celibate does not mean that the priest becomes less human by "denying himself what comes naturally." Being a celibate means that he directs his love through God to others instead of through his own family to others. Living this kind of life does not mean that the priest will love less or that he will be loveless but that, as he gives the power of his procreative love to God, his love will be focused not on his own family but on the family of God and, in turn, he will be loved and cherished by them. As we know in the Roman Church we call our priests "father," not only because through their ministry we are given spiritual life but also because there really is a familial attachment we have to them. Again we see the close familial bond people hold for their priests. This spiritual fatherhood calls the priest to the same degree of faithfulness and selfless love for the people of his parish as the Sacrament of Matrimony calls spouses to faithfulness and selfless love of one another and their children. This kind of love, which both those who are called to Matrimony and those who are called to Holy Orders commit themselves to, is what St. Paul speaks so eloquently of in the thirteenth chapter of his second letter to the Corinthians. In a very real sense the parish priest is "married" to the Church. For the celibate parish priest his "spouse" is the people his serves.

Being a celibate does not mean that the priest is a "clerical" bachelor. This, however, can be and many times is a real temptation for the priest. In reality, no one person is completely dependent upon his constant care. So he can succumb to a real selfishness both emotionally and financially. When this happens his celibacy is in jeopardy. As the saying goes, " A rich celibate is like an overweight sprinter." The antidote for this kind of selfishness is for the priest to tithe. This may seem odd at first but tithing is just as important and essential, maybe more so, for the priest as it is for everyone. I say that tithing is maybe even more important for the parish priest because, since he does not have a wife and family to financial support, he may have more "discretionary funds" at his disposal. The more money and possessions a diocesan priest has, the greater are the chances that they will "take possession" of him. Unless the parish priest tithes it will become increasingly difficult for him to live a life of celibate love. When tithing becomes a way of life for him, every other area of his life will be in the proper order, because when we tithe we are putting God first in our lives. As was mentioned in the chapter about the differences between an order priest and a diocesan priest, the diocesan priest receives a salary and, perhaps, other monetary compensations, for example, royalties on books. It is his obligation to the Lord to give back a tithe, 10%, of what he has been given. Granted, many priests do not tithe. (Could that be the reason their people never hear about the need to tithe on their income and about the spiritual and material benefits God attaches to it?) Their reasoning behind not tithing is—I write this with great authenticity because this is the reason I used until I was finally, and thankfully, "converted" to tithing—"I've given my entire life to God. Surely, He doesn't want part of the measly salary I make!" This attitude can lead to a life of miserly misery for the priest and for anyone with whom he comes into contact. When we tithe, and this "we" includes the diocesan priest, we allow God's generosity to flood every aspect of our life. This "flood of generosity" is critical for the priest to fully live out his call to celibacy.

Living the celibate life also includes the way the priest spends his time. Again, since he does not have a wife and children who would require a great deal of his time and attention, there is always the temptation to be selfish with his time. In over-compensating for his need to "take care of himself and carve out some private time," he might fall prey to becoming the "professional," keeping "bankers' hours" and "seeing people" only when it fits into his schedule. God help the individual who just happens to drop in to see father without an appointment or who cannot come during "office hours." Granted, no one, including the parish priest, needs to be, or for that matter should be, at the beck and call of everyone all the time. But there is a great difference between the priest having to be "on call 24/7" and his being available for his people. The parish priest needs to remember that he is a priest not a businessman, and that the place in which he ministers, not works, and is a parish not a business! Being celibate, especially for a parish priest, allows for this availability.

When a parish priest begins to become exclusive in his relationships, stingy with his money, or selfish with his time, these are indications that there is something out of order in his commitment to living a life of celibacy for God's people and for the sake of God's Kingdom.

Chapter Three:

BELONGING AND SUPPORT

Although the parish priest has no spouse or children of his own, because he is still a very human being he, like every other person, needs intimacy in his life. There have been many psychological studies done showing that a human will die emotionally, and sometimes even physically, depending upon the age of the individual, if he does not have intimacy in his life. By intimacy these studies do not mean a genital sexual relationship. What they do mean is that the person is accepted and cherished by another or by others for who he is, not for what he does. Included in this definition is that this kind of relationship is mutual. In other words, the cherishing and acceptance, the truthful self-revelation and trust go both ways. Intimacy is vital for a person's emotional growth. It is essential for the health and welfare of everyone. It is just not "nice if you can get it." Without intimacy in one's life there is not just something lacking. Without intimacy, one is not fully the human person God created or intended him to be. Where, then, does the celibate priest find this kind of intimacy, which he needs if he wants to be the person God intends him to be? There are three groups of people from whom his intimate relationships will come: family, friends in the priesthood, and friends in the laity.

First we will consider his family. The priest soon realizes that, although he may be called on to witness family weddings and baptize the children of any number of family members, even though he is ordained he is first and last son, brother, nephew, or cousin—not priest. His relationship to his family can be compared to that of a doctor with his family. A doctor usually does not operate on his own family members because of objectivity, or the lack thereof. So, too, the priest with his family members. Keeping this as his "m.o.," he is then free to be son, brother, nephew, and cousin. The point is, the priest needs to have this kind of familial relationship because, hopefully, from his family is where some of the intimacy he needs will come. With his family he does not have to be "the priest who has all the answers." In family gatherings he does not have to be "on." He can simply be son, brother, nephew, and cousin. It is the exception when a family does not accept and love him in this way. Unfortunately, it is also the exception when the priest allows his family to love him in this way. There are many reasons, excuses, for this on the priest's part; but it comes down, in most instances, to the fact that he does not want to seem weak in front of his family or he does not want to worry them or burden them with his problems. Maybe this attitude is ingrained in the male psyche in general, but it can be exacerbated by the "image" the priest thinks he needs to present—even to his own family members. It is very important for the diocesan priest to work on family relationships and to make every effort to keep connected with family members. His family understands his responsibility to his parishioners and that he is "on call" much of the time, but the priest needs to guard against using these as excuses for absenting himself from family gatherings when, in truth, he just does not want to be bothered. He needs to make a real effort to be at birthdays and anniversaries as well as the high holidays and holy days; and, if, especially because of distance, he cannot be there in person, the priest needs to keep in touch via phone, e-mail, or letter. He needs to show them that being a part of the family is very important to him and that they and what goes on in their lives are important to him. Being in close relationships with his family will help him be more compassionate and merciful and understanding with his people, and will help him avoid the tendency of becoming aloof, which can happen to anyone, especially the priest, who isolates himself from the "everyday-ness" of life. Remaining an integral part of his family will go a long way in helping the parish priest be a first-person participant in life instead of being a critical, objective observer. It will help him keep off of the sidelines and on the field.

After his relationship with his family the next most important group for the diocesan priest to form close ties with is his priest brothers. As the time honored saying goes, "You can choose your friends but not your family," obviously and especially because of differing personalities and life interests, the priest will not be equally close to every priest in his diocese. For numerous reasons he will be closer to some and simply be an acquaintance to others. That a parish priest finds and develops close personal relationships with some of his brother priests is essential for his continuation in the ministry and for his own personal growth and emotional health. The parish priest cannot be a "lone wolf" and thrive as a person and continue to be an effective "man of God" for his people. There is no one who can understand a priest better than another priest. Many of his close relationships with fellow priests begin while he is in the seminary; some are formed with those he has lived with in his various diocesan assignments, and some come truly as a gift straight from God Himself. As with the relationships he has with his family members, those with his brother priests take time and effort. Obviously, good lasting relationships done not just happen overnight. They grow and become strong through the years as the trust level deepens. To allow himself to be known and accepted for who he is by a brother priest is truly a gift beyond all price. When a priest finds that kind of fraternal love he needs to do all he can to cherish and nurture it.

For many parish priests this kind of fraternal intimacy is found in priest support groups. There are several varieties of these groups. I would like to single out one in particular because I and four other diocesan priests have belonged to it for the past 30 years. It is called the Jesus Caritas Fraternity. This priest support group is an international fraternity, composed mainly of diocesan priests, formed around the spirituality of Brother Charles deFoucald. Charles was an ex-military man from France who returned to the Sahara desert to live with and to minister to the nomadic people. He founded the Little Sisters and Brothers of Jesus and truly lived almost as a hermit among the desert people. He was killed by a group of nomadic extremists, but his ministry continues to this day in the Sahara. Basically, those who belong to this Fraternity commit themselves to meet once a month for a day of prayer with their group. It is recommended that a group be no larger than six members. The members need to be priests but not necessarily the same age or with the same kind of priestly experience. During their monthly time together, usually the better part of a day, they begin by praying part of the Liturgy of the Hours, the specific "hour" prayed depends upon the time of day they meet. This is followed by an opportunity for them to celebrate the Sacrament of Reconciliation. An essential part of their time together is an hour of adoration before the Blessed Sacrament. Another important aspect of their "day" is what is called the "review of life." This is the time during which each of the brother priests tells his "fact" for the past month. The "fact" is what has been going on in his life that he needs prayer for or discernment with. It really is reflecting out loud before his brothers how God is acting in his life at the present time. After each one shares his "fact" there usually is some quiet prayer before the group addresses what has been said. It is obvious that what is said in the group stays in the group so that over the years the trust level grows increasingly deeper with each meeting. The commitment to each other and to the monthly day of prayer is essential for the continuing growth of the group. Without this commitment to the day and to the necessary confidentiality, a fraternity will not last. It is also recommended that before the monthly meeting each member makes a "day in the desert." This "day" is to be one of quiet meditation, reflecting upon what the Lord is doing in the priest's life during the month and then what "fact of life" he needs to bring before his brothers during their day of prayer together. Many fraternities share a meal on their day and most go on retreat together every other year. Another "commitment" which the fraternity brothers make is to be available to their brother priests, both diocesan and order, who serve in their diocese. A Jesus Caritas Fraternity is not exclusive but inclusive in their relationships with other priests. They are encouraged to live a life of simplicity and to devote themselves to an hour each day in adoration of the Blessed Sacrament. In all honesty I have to say that without the prayerful support, challenge, and encouragement of my fraternity brothers I would not be in active ministry today. That is how essential a support group can be! Truly, after a few years together, your Jesus Caritas Fraternity brothers know you better than you know yourself. What a gift that is for anyone! What an essential gift that is for a diocesan priest!

In addition to a support group, the diocesan priest needs other priests who share like interests to spend some of his free time with, especially on his day off. It is not healthy for a priest to spend all of his days off alone. Granted, depending upon his personality, he may need time to be alone every now and then; but, if he spends his days off mostly alone, there is a tendency for him to become isolated. Again, getting together with some of his brother priests just for some relaxation and enjoyment provides him the opportunity he needs where he does not have to weigh everything he says and where he knows he is accepted for who he is and not for the position he holds. Again, these types of relationships with his brother priests tend to continue not only to keep him connected to his fellow priests but they also help him continue to grow in the realization that being a priest is not a job but a way of life. Who better to help him with this than other priests?

Finally we need to consider the parish priest's relationship with the laity. This relationship presents him with the most challenges because there are differing degrees of acquaintanceship and friendship that require some monitoring to assure that they continue to be healthy for everyone involved. There has been much written and even more discussion about "personal boundaries" in relationships these days regarding doctor-patient, counselor-client, and especially priest-parishioner. With the sexual misconduct controversy involving some priests here in our country, the whole climate regarding how a priest relates with the laity has changed. Especially, the parish priest could become a little paranoid about how his interacting with anyone, in particular with a minor, could be misinterpreted. This dis-ease in priest-laity relationships could lead to a very unhealthy and even to an adversarial future between pastor and parishioner. This would be extremely unfortunate. Both parties would lose and the entire Church would be weakened. The proper response on the part of the priest and the laity to avoid this catastrophe is to face it head on. The priest needs to have a healthy relationship and support from his family and his brother priests. If he has those two relationships in place, then he can have good and healthy relationships with his parishioners and with other lay people. If he does not have those first two relationships in place, he puts any relationship he may have with the laity in jeopardy. When he does not receive the support and the intimacy he needs from his family and his brother priests, he will look for them to be met by his lay friends. When this happens the relationships with the laity are not healthy ones. However, when these first two relationships are healthy, then the relationships the parish priest has with his parishioners and with his other lay friends and acquaintances will also be not only healthy but a real gift to everyone involved. It is part of our reality that, in the course of our lives, we will have many acquaintances and that the number of people we will regard as true friends will be less. This holds true especially for the parish priest. His parishioners become very attached to him because of how he has touched their lives, i.e., baptizing their children, marrying and/or burying their family members, counseling them during times of crisis, celebrating special family events. All of these create a significant and real bond that lasts in many instances for a lifetime. What a blessing this is all the way around! The parish priest really is a "part of every family" because of these things. The majority of these relationships, though, are really acquaintanceships not friendships. This is not to diminish the importance of these relationships in the priest's life or in the life of the people he has touched in these ways. It is simply a matter of looking at them realistically. A priest cannot possibly be a real friend to everyone he helps or comes into contact with. Again, this does not diminish his effectiveness or his love or concern for them. This is just a matter of fact. This being said, there will be people down through his years that the priest will truly become friends with. These will be a true gift from God to him as he will be to them. Although few in number, they will be used by God as a source of comfort and caring, of support and belonging, and of acceptance and challenge for the parish priest. He will feel "at home" with them and he will know that they will always tell him the truth and keep him honest and human. This kind of relationship is really a "gift beyond all price." The wonderful thing is that God *does* send those people into the priest's life. He does not have to go looking for them.

As we have discussed in a previous chapter, the very vocation of the diocesan priesthood means that the parish priest does not live "in community" as the religious or Order priests do. Nevertheless, because one of the most basic needs of every human being is to belong and not to live in isolation, the diocesan priest also needs a "community" in which he can grow and thrive and in which his basic human need for intimacy can be met.

So, it is not just serendipitous if, by chance, he stumbles upon some sort of community life. It is essential for him as a human being and also as a parish priest. Without this "community," made up of equal parts of his own family, his priest brothers, and his friends in the laity, he will not only suffer as a person but he will also not be a very effective parish priest. Without belonging to and being supported by this kind of community, the man will not be able to continue as a diocesan priest.

Chapter Four:

Holy Boldness

All that we have considered so far brings us now to the most important quality a diocesan priest needs to truly be "God's man" for the people he is sent to serve. The quality is boldness. In fact it is more than just a quality. For the parish priest, this quality of boldness needs to be elevated to the status of a virtue. What the man needs to carry out what will be asked of him as a diocesan parish priest down through his years of ministry is the virtue of "holy boldness." Holy Boldness is literally *the* "cardinal," i.e., "hinge," virtue that enables the priest to be the leader God has called him to be. Without this virtue a parish priest has a tendency to be either a "sacrament machine" or a clerical "cruise director." If the former prevails, all that is really necessary is that he "show up" to "do" the sacraments, and as long as he follows the book so that everything is valid and licit "nobody gets hurt and we can get this over with and get on with our lives." When the latter kicks in his main goal is to "keep everybody happy until Jesus comes again." Obviously, these examples are overstated, but the underlying attitude of both shows a lack of holy boldness. So, of what does this very necessary "virtue" consist? Because the diocesan priest, and in particular a parish priest, and most specifically a pastor, is called by his ordination to be shepherd and leader of his people, this holy boldness gives him the strong foundation he will need to fulfill that call. It is made up of the following qualities: speaking the truth of Jesus Christ to his people; having a vision for how the Gospel message will be lived out in the parish; not being afraid of making decisions and carrying them out; being able to work with many leadership groups and various age groups; and encouraging, promoting, and facilitating full, conscious, active, participation in all aspects of parish life.

Speaking the Truth of Jesus to His People:

This quality of speaking the truth of Jesus Christ to his people may seem to be a given for any priest, and, granted, it should be. However, because the priest is as human as the next person, he is greatly tempted at times to tell his people what they want to hear instead of what they need to hear. It is extremely tempting to want to be "nice" so that he does not offend anyone and so that, consequently, he will be liked by everyone. This, as was pointed out above, is the "cruise director" model of the parish priest. The basic difficulty with this model is that Jesus, Himself, was not "nice." Had He been "nice" He would never have been crucified because He would have always told people exactly what they wanted to hear. He was not nice! He told the people the truth of God, His Father. This was why He came to earth. This was the Good News. This was the beginning of our salvation and He laid down His life for this Truth. Many did not want to hear it then and many do not want to hear it now. Because, then as now, many people are not living the truth and so they do not want to be reminded of what they are not doing or of what they are doing that they should not. Speaking the truth of God, preaching the Good News, is what the parish priest is called to do. This is not an easy task—and never has been. He needs to remember, however, that being a priest is not a popularity contest. To paraphrase a popular bumper sticker: "The priest who dies being liked the most does <u>not</u> win!" When he stands before the Good Lord he will not be asked how many people liked him. He will be asked whether he told his people the Gospel truth. Speaking God's truth to his people without watering it down may not be very popular at times; but, as we are told by Jesus, Himself, the truth, and only the truth, will set us free. Above all else the parish priest needs to be about the task of setting his people free, even if his people "crucify" him for telling them what they need to hear instead of what they want to hear. In his homilies, he needs to preach this Gospel of Truth. He means that he has to avoid using the homily as his "bully pulpit" and that he needs to be careful not to just give his "opinions" or to preach the "gospel" according to himself. Being called to preach the Gospel is truly a gift given to him through the laying on of hands, i.e., ordination. When the priest is preaching the Gospel and challenging his people to live their lives according to the truth of Jesus, he certainly needs to be kind and compassionate in his delivery, "not lording it over them as the pagans do." He also needs to be merciful and loving, realizing that he, too, is a sinner in need of God's mercy and love. When he carries out this sacred task, the priest is practicing the virtue of holy boldness.

Having A Vision and Direction for the Parish

As we have said the parish priest is the spiritual leader for his people. Part of this spiritual leadership consists in providing a vision for the parish. This "vision" is not a supernatural apparition. It is really the "direction" in which the parish will go. It is imperative that the pastor establish this for his people. Just as there is one father for a family, so, too, there is one pastor for the parish. If or when a pastor abdicates this part of his responsibility, the parish is truly set adrift because he is not exercising the grace of office he was given when the bishop appointed him pastor and shepherd. He certainly arrives at this vision or direction after much prayer and reflection, and with the help of many from the parish, especially from those in leadership positions, e.g., parish council and school board members. Nevertheless, it is the pastor himself who has the ultimate responsibility to say, in so many words, "This is where we're headed and this is how we're going to get there." This can be one of the greatest challenges for the parish priest. It will mean that, perhaps, some will disagree with the vision or direction and so he will have to deal with criticism. It will also mean that he will have to be not only giving the commands but also "leading the charge" to bring the vision to fruition. Truly, being the pastor of any parish is not for the faint of heart. But this is part of what it is to be a leader—especially a spiritual leader. To lead with vision, the priest needs to have the deep and ever-growing personal spirituality that was discussed in a previous chapter. Without it he will not be able to provide the solid vision and direction every parish needs to bring the Good News to its people. This part of holy boldness requires the virtues of courage, strength, perseverance, and patience, but most of all, and above all, it requires on the part of the parish priest, a tremendous amount of trust in the Lord. Another aspect of setting a vision and direction for the parish is that of not being afraid to make a decision. We will take a closer look at decision-making in the following section of this chapter.

Working with Groups and Individuals

If a priest does not like to work with people he should not be a diocesan priest, and, in particular, he should not be a parish priest. If he abhors having his schedule interrupted, the diocesan priesthood is not for him. Especially in a parish, the priest's usual ministry is one of interruptions. Some of the best and most effective work a parish priest does comes as a result of his schedule being interrupted. I am in no way advocating that he should throw out his appointment book, but I am saying that he should be flexible enough so that he does not become a slave to it. In the ideal world everyone who needs to or wants to speak with a priest should make an appointment a month or two in advance, as he would to see his doctor or lawyer or money manager. A parish is not situated in the ideal world, and the priest needs to remember that he is not his parishioners' doctor or lawyer or money manager; he is their priest. He is not their slave but he is there to serve their spiritual needs; but, like death, most times people cannot schedule when they will need to call upon him for his advice or prayer or absolution. The parish priest learns sooner or later, and we hope sooner, in his life that his people are truly more important than his schedule. Many times people come to their priest because they do not know whom else to turn to. That kind of need cannot be scheduled. Granted, there may be instances where the priest cannot help the person himself. Many times he will have to refer the person to someone else but, at least, he took the time to listen! Holy boldness necessarily includes not only compassion but also, many times, self-denial on the priest's part.

This compassion and self-denial also come into play as the parish priest works with the various parish groups, committees, and organizations. Especially as the constitutions and documents of the Second Vatican Council are continuing to be implemented, collaborative ministry is essential to parish life. One of the important things a pastor does for his parish is to encourage his people to use their God-given talents in service to their community and to continue to call people into the many ministries needed in the parish. The pastor, through his sacrament of Holy Orders, truly "orders," i.e., helps shape, nurture, and prioritize, all of these parish ministries. This does not happen in a vacuum nor does it happen unilaterally. It is his responsibility to call leaders from the parish community to be his advisors in all of these matters. Pastors' advisory councils, parish councils, school boards, finance committees are just some examples of what it takes to help a parish not only run smoothly but also assist in the ongoing process of listening to and then assessing the parish's needs. The parish, as the Church itself, is not now and never will be a democracy. Jesus did not set it up that way. That being said, the parish does not "belong" to Father any more than it is the sole possession of any or all of the parishioners. The necessity for continual dialogue among the pastor and his staff and his parishioners is an essential part of collaborative ministry. Without it the parish will either become a dictatorship, "Whatever Father says goes. I'm the pastor and you're not!" or it will fall into chaos where little "kingdoms" are built by well-meaning people who cannot see the whole picture. Either way the parish will suffer, and the proclamation of the Good News of Jesus Christ, which is the mission of every parish, will be stifled or muted as the battle for parish "turf" begins.

An extremely important aspect of holy boldness is that of not being afraid to make the difficult decisions. Yes, the pastor needs to consult with and remain in dialogue with his staff and parishioners, and especially with the leadership of the parish, but there will come a time when consultation needs to cease on a particular matter and a decision made. The final decision rests with the pastor because he is ultimately responsible for the parish. When a pastor abdicates this part of his role the parish will suffer because, in most instances, someone else, who does not have the grace of office, will then make the decision. When this takes place the parish is "out of order." Many times a pastor will decide <u>not</u> to decide. This is also harmful because the one whose responsibility it is to given fundamental and ultimate direction to the parish is not giving it and so his people become "like sheep without a shepherd." Again, being a "successful" parish priest is not a popularity contest. The "success" of anyone including a priest needs to be measured by how he fulfills the responsibility God has given him. To really "succeed" as a parish priest the man will need to practice holy boldness whereby he steps out "in faith," realizing that God is with him; whereby he trusts in God first and last; whereby he listens to God first and foremost; and whereby he gives the people entrusted to him by that same God vision and direction, challenge and compassion, guidance and courage, and above all else the love and truth of God Himself. This is what holy boldness can and will do for the parish priest. What a difference this makes in the life of a parish!

Promoting Full, Conscious, and Active Participation in the Life of the Parish

Since the end of the Second Vatican Council in 1965 there have been many "images" of the Church proposed, discussed, and implemented. There have also been, although to a lesser degree, many "images" which have attempted to explain the relationship that a pastor or parish priest needs to have with his people so that the Constitutions and Decrees of that Council could be lived out in the community. One of the primary goals of Vatican II that is written about in several of the consiliar documents is that the faithful, in all areas of parish life, have full, conscious, and active participation. For many being "Catholic" simply means, "putting in your time" at Sunday Mass. For many of those people "full, conscious, active participation" translates into "half, unconscious, passive observation" especially at Mass and most likely in all other areas of their daily lives. Because some of his congregation is made up of this type of individual, the priest certainly needs a large "dose" of holy boldness so that he can put across the reality that being Catholic is not a "spectator" sport, either at Mass on Sunday or during the other days of the week. With this in mind, the image of the parish priest that seems to best facilitate the implementation of this full, conscious, active participation on the peoples' part is that of the "conductor of the symphony." First of all, before one note of the symphony is played, all of the orchestra members need to be present and they need to know what part they play. Not everyone plays the oboe or drums or violin; but without each instrument, no matter how seemingly insignificant, the symphony would not be as full and complete as it could and should be—the way the composer wrote it. Who is the one to make certain that all are present and all know their different parts? The conductor. This is the same type of responsibility the parish priest has to his people. He is the one to call them together, especially at Sunday Mass, and it is also his task to make certain they realize the talent each individual has to bring to the service of the community, again especially at Sunday Mass. The conductor encourages the members of the symphony to put their whole heart into playing the particular piece of music in front of them. So, too, the priest encourages his people to enter into whatever God has called them to do with all their heart, mind, and soul. The conductor brings out every nuance of the musical score by giving the orchestra the proper direction that is sometimes so slight and imperceptible the audience does not see it. Similarly, the pastor's touch and influence on his people should be such that even the most challenging and complicated work of the parish appears to flow smoothly to those observing from outside. The most important job of the conductor, however, is to put all of the music each member plays together in such a way that the result is melodious. The pastor, in the same way, because he sees the big picture of what the parish needs to accomplish, coordinates or "orders" all of the various gifts and talents of his parishioners into one harmonious "song of praise" to the Lord in service to the community. Without a conductor who takes his responsibility seriously the orchestra would have no leader, and so each would simply play his instrument however and whenever he wanted. The result would be a cacophony instead of a symphony. Likewise with a parish, when the pastor does not give direction to his people. Everyone ends up "doing his own thing," and what should be a united effort at building up God's Kingdom here on earth turns into a battle over whose individual little "kingdom" gets to use the coffee pot this weekend!

When a parish priest, especially if he is the pastor, embraces his role as shepherd and spiritual leader of and for his people, wonderful things begin to happen. When he relies on his "grace of office" and trusts in the Lord, that He is never outdone in generosity, he is really allowing the Lord to use him in ways that the priest, himself, may have never dreamed of. When this kind of grace-filled action becomes his way of life, his parish begins to explode with God's Spirit and is transformed into a beacon of light and truth and hope for the entire community. This is what happens when the priest dares to practice holy boldness. The virtue spreads into the lives of everyone. Fear is gone. Timidity vanishes; and so the Gospel, the Good News of Jesus Christ, is not only preached by word but, more importantly, by action—and, therefore, becomes **real**!

Chapter Five:

The Effect of Holy Boldness

This "virtue" of holy boldness, I believe, is given by the Holy Spirit to the man at his ordination, along with all of the other gifts he will need to serve God's people as a priest of the High Priest, Jesus Christ. However, just like all of those other gifts, unless it is used on a regular basis, holy boldness will weaken and become dormant. As this happens the priest may succumb to the ever-present temptation of priestly competition or, worse yet, jealousy. The mutual respect that should be a "given" among his fellow priests will also disappear and be replaced by criticism, rumor, and the ever-so-prevalent clerical gossip. There will be divisions between old and young clergy. Labels of conservative and liberal will be assigned and sides will be chosen and battle lines drawn. All of this happens when the priest forgets that it really is "the same Spirit but different gifts" at work in his brothers. This mind-set can always be avoided by practicing holy boldness because this gift, which is there for the asking, focuses on the power of God Himself and upon His promise that He will be with us always until the end of time and that He will never be outdone in generosity. When he practices holy boldness, the priest is very much aware that God is God and he is not. Holy boldness helps put everything into the proper perspective. It allows the priest to see the situation as God sees it and so prevents him from manipulating it according to his own designs. Holy boldness also assists the priest as he interacts with his people, especially with those he may consider bothersome, because it allows him to see everyone as God sees them—as His dear children. The more he practices this virtue, the more the priest will also become aware and believe that he, too, is a precious child of God, His Father.

One of the greatest challenges the diocesan priest faces is his relationship with the priests he will serve with during his years of ministry. Contrary to what many of us were taught in the seminary, there is no "one size fits all" when it comes to those whom God has called to the priestly ministry. So, he needs to realize immediately that, although they are ordained, these men are very human with all of their successes and failures, triumphs and defeats, and especially with all of their differing personalities. Therefore, just naturally, the priest will be attracted by one personality type and be put off by another. There is no way that he can be a real friend to all of his brother priests, just as he cannot be a true friend to everyone in his parish. However, the fraternity of the priesthood is a real one that needs to be nurtured by every priest. This simply means that—and holy boldness helps this happen—there is mutual respect among the brothers. Pettiness, backstabbing, rumors, and gossip have no place within the ranks of the priesthood. This also means that everyone should rejoice in the successes and achievements of their brothers instead of being jealous or envious. They need to truly learn from one another instead of being in constant competition. Above all else sarcasm and cynicism have no place in this fraternity. These two "demons" wreck havoc on everyone they touch. They are the cause of suspicion and they are the destroyers of trust among the brothers. Holy boldness is the antidote because it helps the priest "rejoice with those who rejoice and weep with those who weep," especially when "those" are his brother priests.

When practiced, holy boldness allows the Holy Spirit to "shine" through this "vessel of clay," as Archbishop Fulton J. Sheen referred to himself. With all of his faults and shortcomings, and probably because of them and not in spite of them, the man who is a priest is chosen by the High Priest, Jesus Christ, to act as His instrument of salvation for the people. When holy boldness is practiced, the words of Sacred Scripture: "You have not chosen Me but I have chosen you," ring in his ears; and the priest is reminded that it is not he alone who acts. He is acting in the place and person of Christ Jesus Himself. When holy boldness becomes **the** way of life for him, the priest understands what John the Baptist meant when he said of Jesus, "He must increase and I must decrease." Holy boldness helps the priest remember that it really is all about Jesus and not about him! Holy boldness leads the priest to true humility, true honesty before the Lord. It helps him to never be "puffed-up" or "deflated" because with this "virtue" comes the ability to focus on God's mercy and holiness instead of on his own sinfulness and the tendency that he, like everyone else, has to compare himself to others, especially to other priests. With holy boldness God Himself is the focus of the priest's every action. Like Our Blessed Mother, when he practices holy boldness, the priest becomes the "magnifying glass" of God. He makes God clearer and nearer for his people.

Is there a downside to holy boldness? Yes. It is the same "downside" that Jesus Himself experienced. As was discussed in a previous chapter, just as Jesus was literally crucified for boldly speaking the truth of His Father as he told the people what they needed to hear and not necessarily what they wanted to hear, so too will the priest be figuratively "crucified" for his boldness in proclaiming the same truth. The reality of every priest's situation is that, no matter what he does or says, there will always be some who will criticize. If this is the situation, and it certainly is, is it not better and ultimately more beneficial for the priest to be criticized for speaking the truth? In a word, YES! In the final analysis the main effect holy boldness has on the priest is to set him free to practice his ministry as God has called him to do, not with temerity and tentativeness, but with courage and conviction underscored by mercy and compassion. The effect that holy boldness will have on his people will be to encourage them also to put it into practice as they live out their faith in the workplace, and especially in their families. The Holy Spirit has not given any of us a spirit of being timid but of boldly proclaiming with all of our strength the Good News of Jesus Christ! What a gift it is to our world and how blessed are we when we put it into practice!

EPILOGUE

This book is neither the first nor last that deals with the subject of the spirituality of the diocesan priest. My hope is that it will be part of the discussion and that it will bring some clarity and give some direction to both the laity and to my brother priests, both diocesan and religious order men, in this vast area which composes our spiritual lives. As a result of reading this book, my sincere hope is that you pray for your priests, if you belong to the laity, and, if you belong to the clergy, that we pray for each other—and that all of us pray for the Church, especially for our bishops. This, as we all are very aware, is a very challenging time for us Catholics! As the old Chinese curse states: "May you live in interesting times." For our Church these are very interesting times. We know, however, through the gift of our faith and by trusting in Our Lord, that He will never abandon us. He will, on the contrary, be with us always "until the end of time." We believe with all our hearts that "nothing is impossible with God," and so we are confident that He will again, as He has in every age of the Church, write straight with our crooked lines. With this in mind, I offer two meditation prayers: one for our lay brothers and sisters for their priests; and one for priests, for ourselves and for our brothers.

God, Our Loving Father, I present to You all of our priests, especially those who minister in our parish. Give them the strength, dear Lord, to speak Your truth to us whether it disturbs us or not. Give them the courage to practice Holy boldness in all of their dealings with us so that Your truth will shine through their every action. Deliver them, Lord, from the spirit of temerity and fill them with the strength of Your courage! I ask that you give them the comfort and the consolation of Your peace and joy so that they will know in their heart of hearts that what they are saying and doing is Your holy Will.

Give them also, dear Lord, the spirit of humility so that they may know and see themselves as you know and see them, as Your precious children, ones whom You have called and chosen to be Your men for us. Lord, I ask You to lead them along the path of holiness so that they, in turn, will lead me on that same path. Bring them, at last, into the glory of the Kingdom which you have prepared for your good and faithful shepherds.

Dear Lady, Queen of the Clergy, I ask you also to pray for our priests. Keep them pure in body, mind, and heart. Give them your gift of obedience. Be a mother to them always, bringing them ever closer to Your Son, the High Priest, so that when they celebrate the Sacraments for us, especially the Holy Eucharist, it will be truly the person of Jesus Himself in them. May they, like You, always bring the Holy Trinity clearer and nearer to all of us.

I ask these blessings for them, dear Father, in the name of Jesus, Your Son, and our Saving Lord.

AMEN.

God, Our Loving Father, I, a priest of Your Son, Jesus the Christ, pray for Myself and for all of my brother priests, especially for those who work in parish ministry. Give us, dear Lord, a spirit and heart to serve and love your people as did Your Son. Instill within us, as you did for your servant, the Prophet, Elisha, a "double portion" of Your gift of holy boldness. Allow us the courage and strength to be true leaders and shepherds of your people. Help us to preach by word and example, in season and out, the Truth of the Gospel, proclaiming the Good News to all. As part of this "double portion," keep constantly in our minds and hearts the realization of our own need for Your mercy, forgiveness, compassion, and healing as we minister to those whom You send us, especially as we minister to our parishioners.

Help us not look upon our weakness, but upon the strength of Your Call in our lives so that we may always remember whose Kingdom we proclaim. With all of our heart, until our last breath, may we believe Your Word that we read, teach what we believe, and practice what we teach.

But most of all, dear Father, may we imitate what

we handle, Your Son, Jesus Christ, Our Eucharist Lord. And when our bodies finally wear out in Your service and we appear before Your Throne make us worthy to celebrate with all of the angels and saints that heavenly Liturgy which lasts for all eternity!

Dear Mary, Mother and Queen of priests, pray for us. Ask your Spouse, the Holy Spirit to strengthen our resolve to live pure and obedient lives. Share with us how you lived in the world while remaining detached from it. Be a mother to us especially in times of temerity and temptation. Help all that we do give honor and glory to God alone; and may we proclaim with our lives, as you did with yours, the greatness of the Lord. Bring us always and ever closer to Your Son and at the hour of our death take us by the hand and lead us safely home to Him.

I ask these blessing for myself and for my brother priests, dear Father, in the Name, above all names, Your Son, and our Saving Lord, Jesus Christ.

AMEN.